JOSEPH HOWE

& THE BATTLE

FOR FREEDOM

OF SPEECH

*

Sir.

— Living as we do in a free and intelligent Country, and under the influence of a Constitution which attaches to our rulers the salutary restrictions of responsibility in all matters of government, is it not surprising that the inhabitants of Halifax, should have so long submitted to those shameful and barefaced [impositions] which have from year to year been levied on them, in the shape [...] [...]d attempts have from time to time been made, by ind[...] [...]ongst their countrymen some spirit of resist[...] [...]ual exactions, which have been drained from t[...] [...] the torpid indifference to public matt[...] [...]f the people, has at length become qui[...] [...]n what must be their future condition[...] [...]f the State. In a young and poor coun[...] [...]ceive education at the public expence[...] [...] exactions of a few; where the hard earn[...] [...]o repay their ill timed generosity with co[...] [...]men of moderate circumstances and humble [...] [...]t against measures which are fast working the[...] [...]xist in any free state, save Nova Scotia, a respon[...] [...]rs brave and brook the repeated censures of the Pr[...] [...]tion of their conduct, or giving to the public some ex[...] [...]just and licentious libels, which have repeatedly been a d[...] [...]untry. Are the journals of our land exclusive; do they[...] [...] the people, and shut their columns against the sober a[...] [...] I cannot think this, Mr.Howe; and yet weeks have el[...] [...] too plain to be misunderstood, have been plac[...] [...]f the public, and yet no champion of th[...] [...]ly and willingly admit that th[...] esteem and res[...] with the[...] affi[...] 30[...]

JOSEPH HOWE
& THE BATTLE
FOR FREEDOM
OF SPEECH

*

John Ralston Saul

GASPEREAU PRESS ℊ PRINTERS & PUBLISHERS
2006

*This speech was originally delivered at the
University of King's College School of Journalism,
Halifax, Nova Scotia, on 20 March 2004
as the inaugural Joseph Howe Lecture*

THIS YEAR IS Joseph Howe's 200th anniversary and the 25th anniversary of the journalism school here, at King's College. In that context I've been asked to give the inaugural Joseph Howe Lecture, which is also the third Brian Flemming Lecture. Mr. Flemming tells me that he began his lecture series as the direct result of a lecture I gave here a few years ago, lamenting the lack of public debates about ideas and the public good. In other words, a great deal is supposed to happen this morning in a single lecture.

I should add that this is also the first of a series of conferences the journalism school is going to hold twice a year. What for? In order to discuss the context and ethics of journalism, rather than the utilitarian nuts and bolts of journalism.

As you all know, one of the easy temptations in this world—which loves to define progress through measurement—is to turn education into training.

8   This slide towards replacing thought with what can more properly be done through apprenticeship on the job—towards replacing content with methodology—is particularly problematic when it comes to journalism. And so the idea of a twice-yearly conference about content and ethics in journalism is an important initiative.

It is also exciting to know that the next stage in the development of Halifax's journalism program is to be the creation of an annual Joseph Howe Prize for courage in journalism. My suggestion to the advocates of this prize is that it should be national in nature, but it should be anchored absolutely in Halifax. In other words, it should consist of a Nova Scotia jury giving out a national prize.

Quite apart from all of these initiatives, it is exciting for me to be able to spend the day here with all of you, listening to what leading journalists have to say about the situation of investigative journalism in Canada today.

THAT YOU SHOULD ASK someone who has no historic or family links to Halifax or to Nova Scotia to give the inaugural Joseph Howe lecture I take as a very personal honour. The link which I do have to this lecture is a particular admiration for Joseph Howe, despite the fact that in my first major book about Canada—*Reflections of a Siamese Twin*—he really didn't get the attention he was due. My Nova Scotia friends gave me a hard time over this. I then set about reading, reading and reading—nobody ever said that Joseph Howe was a master of brevity—and I soon realized my profound error. It's always a good thing to be happy to admit your errors in public.

Let me add to my now well-founded admiration for Joseph Howe, that I also have a great love for this city and this province. It is a very strong love which predates coming here for official reasons. I think that Halifax is one of the most astonishing cities in the country. In the last quarter century, after many difficulties, this city has reactivated itself and its regional and national role. It has now become, once again, a real, national centre in a great variety of ways. It is a real centre for all of Canada in the arts, in thought, in teaching and in urban planning.

More directly relevant to this lecture, Halifax has been for a very long time and in a very intense way one of the key building sites for Canadian democracy, for the building of freedom of speech and for the enunciation of the idea of freedom of the press.

The first time I came to Halifax, my primary destination was the library inside the Nova Scotia Legislature. In 1835, as Haligonians know, that room in that small beautiful building was the site of the high court. It was there that Joseph Howe gave his six-and-one-quarter-hour defence against charges of

10 criminal libel. Please note that he defended himself without a lawyer.

These charges, were designed to ruin him person-ally, to destroy him financially and to force the collapse of his newspaper, *The Nova Scotian*. This situation resembled strangely the more current phe-nomenon of *libel chill* which, beginning some 15 years ago, was used against writers in Canada for precisely the same reasons.

Many believe, including myself, that in the proc-ess of winning his acquittal, Howe established the fundamental ideas, principles and shapes of freedom of speech and freedom of the press in Canada.

There are many lawyers and legal academics who will argue over the details. They will argue that in the decades following the Joseph Howe trial, the degree and nature of our freedom of speech and the press flowed backwards and forwards. There was a great deal of technical and legal disorder. Some actu-ally see his trial as being not so much about libel as about sedition.

But put aside the technical details. Look at shape and movement. It was Howe who established the intellectual foundation of how we—all of Canada—still struggle to solidify and to widen the nature of freedom of speech and of the press.

To argue that his libel trial could not be the key moment, simply because there was regression after-wards, misses the essential point: freedoms of speech and press are based upon principles and aided by laws, but nevertheless, they need to be defended and indeed reconquered on a day-to-day basis.

The historic link between Howe's defence and the ninth and tenth lines of our Charter of Rights is about as straight and clear as an historic link can possibly be. It's worth emphasizing this detail—freedom of speech is to be found on the ninth and tenth lines of the Charter of Rights. In other words, the guarantee of freedom of speech and freedom of the press is not something added on or rated low in the body of the Charter of Rights. This is the second of the four fundamental guarantees in the Charter and it comes right at the beginning of the text.

THERE ARE A LOT of students in this hall. As I said at the beginning, and I'm sure it is not the case here, in many journalism schools the students spend a great deal of their time on the technical training of how to be a journalist. That is the sort of thing they could learn in six months on the job or spend four years doing in a journalism school. And then they graduate and get a job and discover that most of the technical machinery and technical methodology they were taught is already obsolete. Of course, there's no harm in teaching that sort of stuff briefly, just so students get the idea that there is a technical aspect to journalism.

Far more important, however, is that at journalism

12   school you have the time to be taught and to discuss the underlying nature of the public good, of history, philosophy and politics, and how all of this relates to journalism. These are the hardest things for a practising journalist to get a handle on. You need to get a handle on it before you are employed and find yourself under fire and being pushed from all sides by everything from employers and editors to competing advertisers and politicians. From the first article written, from the first story, you will be put to the test by somebody. Within hours, certainly within the first week, you will begin to discover whether you have the willpower to stand your ground. In other words, you will quickly discover whether you have an ethical core and whether you're willing to stand for the ethics that you think you possess.

If you have not been given four good years at journalism school of intensely trying to understand in a very personal way what an ethical core is and how it relates to your personal and your society's history and politics and constitution, then, when that first ethical test comes, you may find yourself unprepared for what it takes to stand your ground. You may have the desire to do so, but not have the intellectual structure which can help you stand firm. Unless you are a particularly hard person, which most really good journalists are and so by their very character tend to stand firm, you may find this almost impos-

sible. Being nice is not a particularly useful quality in   13
public life. Being tough in order to stand by your ethics is absolutely essential. But since most people are
nicer than they are tough, what you need in order to
help you stand firm is a relatively clear understanding of what ethics is, what the public good is, and
how you serve it by being clear and therefore firm in
your ethical positions.

N OW LET ME RELATE this back to Joseph
Howe. One thing which is little understood
in the rest of Canada—and to some extent it is
not understood in Nova Scotia either—is Howe's
influence on the country as a whole. I think you
could argue that his influence on the creation of
Canada and the idea of Canada goes far beyond the
question of freedom of speech in Nova Scotia and the
work that he did in Nova Scotia.

Let me give you one illustration. Fred Dickson was
the leader of the 1919 Winnipeg strike, along with
J.S. Woodsworth and others. Immediately after the
strike, the leaders were charged with seditious libel.
Fred Dickson was advised by friends to avoid using
a lawyer and instead to defend himself. They sug-
gested that he defend himself in exactly the tradition
and manner of Joseph Howe. That was their specific
reference.

His defence was based entirely on the principle

14 of Joseph Howe's defence. In other words, in the 160 years since Howe gave his speech in this city, public leaders have been reading and rereading it in order to imagine how they themselves might either specifically defend themselves or speak from an ethical centre in their own public lives. When you read Howe's defence, you are reminded "that as the security of life and property was strengthened by the influence of the press, so they would be destroyed beneath the ruins." You can still hear the echo of this rhetoric in Dickson's own defence: "In your hands is placed the question of liberty of speech, whether a man has a right to criticize government officials or not."

Dickson was acquitted, as Howe had been acquit-ted, and in very much the same manner. Following his acquittal, the charges were dropped against the other strike leaders, including J.S. Woodsworth.

Perhaps the reason we don't understand Howe's national influence is because we're distracted by that period of time during which he was, along with Antoine-Aimé Dorion, the leading opponent of Confederation. That opposition was both real and interesting, but it obscures the fact that in an earlier time he had been the original proponent of Confederation. It also obscures the fact that he went on, shortly after Confederation, to become a very important player in the federal cabinet. In any case, his contribution to Canada goes well beyond any particular political stand that he took at a particular time. I'm not arguing that he was right or wrong. I'm just saying that his influence was essential to the way in which Canada conceived of itself.

There is, for example, his role in establishing not simply public education, but public education as the keystone of an egalitarian approach towards democracy in Canada. Howe said: "If you were my brother I would not permit your interests to weigh a feather against a trust so sacred as I believe our public school system to be."

When he came to power in 1848, in the first responsible government in Canada, he and his allies put into place a long list of essential reforms, just as LaFontaine and Baldwin would do in Upper and Lower Canada.

These two governments laid the foundations inside Nova Scotia and Canada for what would become the best of the Canadian idea.

Their reforms included laws relating to public probity, corruption, honesty, modern electrical communications, railways, the post office. It is not said enough that the creation and expansion of the post office was one of the essential egalitarian acts in the building of democracy. Before the existence of a widespread and reliable post office, you had to have enough money to hire a courier to carry your message. The post office made it possible for citizens to send messages for a reasonable amount of money.

16 And communications, as we all know, is a central element of freedom of speech.

There were also major reforms to the legal system, the establishment of professional civil services and the beginnings of labour codes. All of this was made possible because of the initial victory of responsible government, which is to say the establishment of the executive half of democracy.

I'm always very conscious when I speak of the role of LaFontaine and Baldwin that, like so many things in Canada, there is actually an essential triangle. If the triangular foundation of Canada is aboriginal, francophone and anglophone, so the essential triangle of Canadian democracy is Howe, LaFontaine and Baldwin.

Not only that. Joseph Howe was one of the primary examples of the east-west nature of the Canadian idea. Many of his disciples moved from Nova Scotia to the Prairies, and onto the Pacific as the nineteenth century wore on. Because they were among the first to devote themselves to political organization in these areas, they also were in a leading position to define the style of democracy adopted. The style of democracy they chose, which we eventually called the Canadian style, was in part defined and shaped by Joseph Howe and his allies in Nova Scotia. They in effect became the leaders of the democratic movement in many parts of Western Canada in the second

half of the nineteenth century. It was they who led
the move towards responsible government, in particular in British Columbia.

Canadians, including British Columbians, tend to
talk about British Columbia as if it were somehow
an isolated entity on the other side of the Rockies.
In fact, B.C.'s two closest allies across the history of
Canada have been, not Britain and not California, but
Nova Scotia and Quebec. Joseph Howe and George-
Étienne Cartier are the patrons or the godfathers of
responsible government, democracy and economic
prosperity in British Columbia.

British Columbia's entry into Confederation was
largely defined and negotiated according to a model
laid out by George-Étienne Cartier. He encouraged
the British Columbia negotiators to ask for a great
deal more than they had first put forward, so that he
would be able to get it for them.

The democratic model was to a great extent
based on Howe's principles. Amor De Cosmos has
often been ridiculed as a mad figure. In fact, he was
a brilliant leader. It was only towards the end, long
after he left power, that he had a mental breakdown.
I've always felt that he was unfairly ridiculed by
those belonging to a political and historical tradition which in the East we would call the anti-democratic *Family Compact*. In British Columbia, this was
called the *Family Company Compact*, the word *company*

18   referring to the Hudson's Bay Company. Amor De Cosmos was a disciple of Joseph Howe and was the leader of the Howites in British Columbia. He always referred to "the great principle of public education." He and his friends understood that in a country as poor and underpopulated as Canada, so dependent on immigration, universal public education equalled democracy. It was not surprising, therefore, that the British Columbia Public School Act of 1872 begins with a description of the obligation of the province to "give every child in the province such knowledge as will fit him to become a useful [and there you think, aha! How utilitarian! But then it goes on] and intelligent citizen in after years." In other words, the noun in this sentence is citizen. The purpose of education is to create citizens.

Howe's approach towards public government always included an obsession with utility and the delivery of modern services. He worked for the expansion of train systems. He worked for the installation of modern communication systems. As in the B.C. School Act, so in his political theories. Thus, the concept of utility was the adjective. The noun was *citizen*. This intellectual and conscious obsession with citizenship can be found again and again in the arguments of Howe, LaFontaine and Baldwin. They saw themselves, in a surprisingly conscious way, as the initiators of a modern, atypical experiment in democratic government; one which was not British, not French, not American. The originality and conscious intellectual origins of our democratic beginnings are as essential today as they were then. They guide us whenever we set about debating what seem to be new choices.

Of course, Howe was filled with contradictions. Why shouldn't he have been? After all, he was engaged in a formative period of public life, as we moved from the status of undemocratic colonies towards the status of an almost democratic nation-state. It isn't all that strange that he should have, at first, proposed Confederation and then opposed it and then worked to build it.

It could be argued that, in spite of this contradiction, his approach towards public life came closer to the ideas of modern Canada than to the ideas held by many of the other early leaders. I'll give you a few examples. First, he was the clearest on the subject of free debate and free speech. His mind had been clarified in the courtroom in 1835: "Yes, gentlemen, come what will. While I live, Nova Scotia shall have the blessing of an open and unshackled press."

Second, he was profoundly anti-ideological. He believed in a balance between individualism and community; opportunity and community; neither the American model nor the European model.

Third, he was very wary, far more wary than Mac-

20 donald, of cheap patriotism. He hated cheap patriotism.

From 1869 to 1870, he was Secretary of State for the Provinces in the government of Canada. As a result he was responsible for bringing Manitoba into Confederation. He was then in his late sixties and not in good health. He went out in the summer of 1869 to visit the Red River Settlement. It took 22 days to get there, a very rough trip; and while there he put in place the elements of a moderate solution to what didn't need to become a problem.

He came back through early winter storms, a terrible return trip which broke his health. He never really recovered. But once in Ottawa he reiterated his belief that there was an easy way to come to a solution; that the Métis, the francophones, the established anglophones and the anglophone Métis could all work together with the new Ontario immigrants to Manitoba; and they could do it without anybody being robbed or done out of what was theirs. Because he spoke up clearly, he was persecuted in a vitriolic and personal manner—the second time in his life after the libel trial—by the *patriotic* press of Upper Canada; the protestant, *patriotic* press.

They used catchy phrases which had no basis in truth. It turned into one of those moments when truth doesn't matter. You could say absolutely anything about Joseph Howe, get away with it, and hope that some of the mud would stick.

It was pure emotional loathing that was thrown at him on a week-by-week basis—hatred, division, personalization. There were accusations that he'd clinked champagne glasses with Louis Riel. Things like that. They were just made up and thrown out in the hope that they could not so much destroy Howe, as ensure that the good Howe had done would be undone. There is always a hint of lunacy once false populism gets the wind in its sails. Champagne in the Red River Settlement! Their aim was to prevent a compromise in Manitoba.

The racists, anti-democrats, false populists and yellow journalists half won and half lost. Howe survived politically. His province stayed loyal to him. The government stayed loyal to him. But it was one of those incredibly unpleasant moments, when everyone seemed to be emotionally out of control. The attack, which began on Joseph Howe in 1870, ended years later with the hanging of Riel.

Howe and indeed Charles Tupper had attempted to put forward a moderate, Maritime-style, non-ideological position. The incapacity of the Canada of that day to remain with that moderate position led eventually to the one truly violent moment which set Canadians to killing Canadians.

22 Now some of you will be surprised to hear me invoking Charles Tupper in the same breath as his political enemy, Joseph Howe. But then perhaps you don't know that Charles Tupper also went out to the Red River Settlement in 1870. He went in order to help his daughter and son-in-law, who were out there, and had somehow been caught up in the tensions. While he was there, the old political pro, needless to say, had meetings with Riel and his supporters. Tupper came back to Ottawa and said that he also understood the moderate position of the Métis. He also felt that there was a way out of what looked in Upper Canada to be an impasse.

So the incapacity of our country to stick with the moderate position put forward by these two great Nova Scotians, and our weakness at giving into the immoderate position of the protestant extremists in Ontario, led by the Orange Order, produced a first great division which almost destroyed Canada. That breakdown foreshadowed future destructive moments in our country. We have seen them repeat themselves from time to time throughout our history. Not too often, yet far too often. If you look carefully, you can see them coming long before they're actually upon us; moments like the anti-bilingual air traffic controller crisis when suddenly anyone could say anything, anything at all, and a great deal of ill will was created and damage done to the country.

When one of these fits of national hysteria get

going, you can immediately sense that by the time it is over a lot of people will be embarrassed by the way in which they have acted; the way in which they have allowed the absence of truth to become a satisfying emotional experience. Nevertheless, these break-downs do seem to come upon us. And each time damage is done. And each time we have to work a little harder in order to smooth over the unpleasant-ness which such experiences lay into our society.

Thucydides said—"If you attack not the objective validity, but the good faith of your opponent, you will introduce an element which will poison demo-cratic proceedings."

Joseph Howe in his libel defence had admitted that he considered himself to be a good family man and that he needed to protect the well-being and reputation of his family. But he refused absolutely to ask for the sympathy of the jury. Instead he insisted that what he was putting in front of them was his public life. He wanted them to judge him on his public life. And he was very clear about both the strength and the necessary limitations of the activi-ties of journalism:

God forbid that I should attempt to set the press above the law. Society should tolerate no privileged class that are not amenable to it. I endeavour so to perform my daily duties that I can at any time come before a jury and jus-tify my conduct if required. If influenced by hatred and

24   malice I publish matter, the tendency of which is injuri-
ous and which is justified by no public necessity, that
may be punished with the utmost rigour of the law. That
if in pursuing my lawful calling I seek the public good,
even if I commit an error of judgement, I have a right to
protection from a jury and from a liberal construction of
the law.

In other words, along with his distrust of cheap
patriotism—something which he showed clearly
at great cost to himself over the Manitoba question—he also had a great distrust of the people who
put forward cheap patriotism. These were the kind
of people he said, who "claimed all the loyalty, all the
intelligence and all the respectability for themselves."
He was a great believer in anti-heroism. He was one
of the founders of that Canadian distrust of heroes
laid out so clearly by George Woodcock in the introduction to his biography of Gabriel Dumont.

As you know, Howe wrote a great deal of poetry.
It's rarely quoted, for a fairly understandable reason.
Nevertheless, I will try to recite to you a few lines
from one of his anti-heroic poems:

> Oh, fame will man ne'er cease to bow the knee
> Before thy bloody shrine and strive to free his spirit
> From thy heavy, galling chain
> Which bows it down to toil and guilt and pain.

You could say that all of Joseph Howe's career was a struggle against fame; a struggle against cheap, false heroism which was always tied to cheap and false patriotism, which in turn was, and indeed is always, tied to a lack of respect for truth and professionalism.

WHY HAVE I BEGUN this talk with so much history? Perhaps because this history remains so remarkably modern. It isn't a day old. It's today's history. It's tomorrow's history.

After all, what have I just described to you? I've described the need for absolute freedom of the press. As a former president of the writers' organization, Canadian PEN, I have always believed in absolute freedom of the press, no matter how peculiar it is at times. And in that context I have always believed in professionalism over both emotion and personalization. It is worth remembering, given how central freedom of speech is to every form of freedom whether literary, political or economic, that PEN is the only international organization built upon an obsession with this right and obligation.

Nevertheless, the existence of broad freedom of speech will always mean the unavoidable existence of a small amount of yellow journalism and false populism. The point in a free society is to avoid even thinking about forbidding or persecuting that

26 irresponsible, unprofessional aspect of journalism. Rather it is to encourage the highest possible standards by the greatest number of journalists. What does that mean? A short list might run as follows: the conscious rejection of the methods of the yellow press, which would mean a minimalizing of personalization and denigration on the one hand and hero worship on the other; the rejection of false populism, which for so much of the twentieth century was the most obvious sign of profoundly anti-democratic political activity; the rejection of cheap patriotism; the rejection of ideology; the ability to remain firmly anchored by ethical positions because you believe that you are attempting to approach a truth, knowing full well that it will always remain strangely elusive; a belief in fairness and even-handedness; and an understanding of the danger of provoking division through enmity.

If we look around at the 20-odd Western democracies, we can see that they are the best-educated societies civilization has ever seen. Of course, we have literacy problems. But there have never been so few people without education. There have never been so many PhDs and MAs. I'm not quite sure what that means. More precisely, I've got a PhD and I'm not sure what it means. In any case, there have never been so many people with so much education.

What's more, we live more than 75 percent longer

than we were living 100 years ago. That means we have a great deal more time. We are not in any rush. In spite of the political disorder outside of the democracies, these 20 countries remain remarkably stable. In fact, we've been stable for over a half century. It's hard to think when this has happened before. Our societies are, of course, filled with flaws. Nevertheless, they are relatively fair by historic standards.

So here we are with high education, long life, stability and fairness. That suggests that there is no need for enmity. No need for false populism. No need for malevolent division or unnecessary division. There is certainly no need for yellow journalism and false populism. And we have another advantage—all this remarkable technology. It doesn't make us think any faster, but it allows us to get the nuts and bolts of life into place a great deal faster than ever before. That means we have even more time to educate ourselves, to live, to be stable, to be fair, and above all to think and to discuss and to argue.

We've never been so free and so available for serious, prolonged, in-depth, complicated public debate. Never before.

And so it is rather surprising to look back at those astonishing moments in the second half of the eighteenth century when Pitt and Burke and Fox in the British Parliament took hours and hours to debate

28 ideas; and the philosophical, ethical underpinnings of those ideas. And there, in the 1830s, 40s, 50s are Howe, LaFontaine and Baldwin debating ideas at great length. They themselves and most of their political friends were going to die young. They didn't have much time. Most of them would be dead before they were 40 or 50. A few made it to 60. And they had to write everything out by hand. Yet they found days and days to debate ideas. And had time left over to carry out a political revolution. Now, here we are living to be 80, 90, 100 and yet, we are virtually incapable—with the exception of periodic meetings like this—of devoting our public life to lengthy debates about ideas. A growing percentage of the space occupied by the media is reduced to phrases of three or four words which don't contain verbs.

Or they are only verbs. An increasing percentage of our media experiences are devoted to little more than primal shouts. Shouts repeated again and again and again. Pulse news, pulsation. Pulsations as opposed to arguments or thought. Clips which are mere seconds long, repeated endlessly, so short and so endlessly that they become interesting in the sense that they are so uninteresting.

Tiny little fractions of ideas endlessly repeated. The exact opposite of a public discussion or debate. Fractions of ideas, shouts completely unattached to context, completely unattached to the possibility of establishing whether what is being discussed has any relationship to truth or to history or to anything else. These short loud shouts are little more than emotion; or the scripted facsimile of emotion. And so nuance becomes more difficult. Manichaeism becomes increasingly prevalent. We are presented with black versus white, good versus evil. Are you for or are you against? Three words in favour, three words against.

Above this shapeless but insistent noise floats a new media aristocracy—Columnists. There are many who write columns of a very high quality. Some of them are with us today. And one of the greatest intellectual and stylistic tests of writing is to be able to provide 1,000 words or 900 words or 750 words twice a week or even more often. How are you to do it in an interesting and complex and fair way? A lot of journalists try very hard. I have a feeling they ruin their family lives trying to do this, because it's tough to have two ideas modulated with nuance in under 1,000 words. And to do this repeatedly.

And so, as in the more common world of pulsation, it is far easier for a columnist to put forward a Manichaean position than a nuanced one. As the percentage of newspaper space taken up by columnists has increased, so Manichaeism has become stronger and nuance has become more difficult. Perhaps this was inevitable. After all, compare the number of

30 words in the most serious television news report with the number in an average column. Both are about the same length as a major news piece in a tabloid. More important, compare the number of words in an average news report on a serious television or radio station with the number in an average news piece in a tabloid. You will find the tabloid report is usually longer than the TV or radio report. The determining question of length is thus set in the classic context of false populism; that is, the news piece in a tabloid. And the tabloid approach is dependent on Manichaeism

The combined effect of a world filled with pulsations and brief opinions is a constant buzz, which in turn produces the illusion of discussion. But the structures of much of our mainstream freedom of speech make it virtually impossible for society to engage in a discussion. Instead what we have is a verbal tennis match of someone's 300 words against another person's 600 words against another person's 750 words. You're not even guaranteed a tennis match. That would require a balance or a variety of opinions. But if the ownership patterns make that less likely, well then, you won't even be given much access to a variety of pulsations. And even if you do have a variety, you're still only watching a tennis match. It's still only a Manichaean match of batting opposites back and forth. That isn't actually relevant to a debate of ideas.

Many of the journalists in this room do the exact opposite. Many of you slog long and hard doing investigative journalism. That's the hardest form of journalism anyone can do. And it's the toughest sort of life. Most of the time, it forces you to remain relatively invisible. Investigative journalism, along with reporting, is the nuts and bolts of real journalism. In many ways, that was what Joseph Howe was doing in the 1830s when he took on the corruption of the magistrates.

This tradition of investigative journalism is still incredibly strong in Canada. It is much stronger than most people realize. I'm lucky enough to see this once a year when the Michener Award is presented. Six stories are chosen as finalists. They may have come to life in newspapers, magazines or on radio or television. Six separate groups of journalists come forward at Rideau Hall, one after the other, and explain what drove them to do their lengthy, complex stories and in what way they managed to change society for the better. And then one of them is chosen as the winner. But all of them agree that any one of the six could well have been chosen. You realize that evening how much serious investigative journalism there is going on in small newspapers, as well as in the big papers and yes, even on the big television channels.

As some of you know, only a few days ago we held the fifth LaFontaine-Baldwin lecture. Last year, it was held here in Halifax and the Chief Justice spoke.

32   This year, it was held in Toronto. In the introduction, I talked about Joseph Howe. And I felt very comfortable doing so in the context of this year's lecturer, David Malouf, the leading Australian writer and the first non-Canadian to give this lecture.

He spoke on a Friday night in front of some 1,300 people. On the Saturday morning, we invited the public to come to another room in order to join in a round-table discussion, which lasted about five hours and was organized around two of the key topics which Malouf had brought up the night before. Last year in Halifax, we began to experiment with a way of doing this. And this year I think we perfected it. The method quite simply is to invite people to sit down at any one of the dozens of round tables in the room. They find themselves in groups of eight to ten. Each table is then chaired by somebody, usually somebody well known. It might be a provincial chief justice or a leading journalist or an historian or a student leader or a university president.

And so people walked in off the street on Saturday morning, sat down, and discovered that they were not going to be passive participants, but would be caught up in an intense conversation chaired by Bob Rae or Haroon Siddiqui or Margaret Conrad or Émile Martel. Suddenly they realized that this was an opportunity to have a real debate with a reasonable number of citizens. What we discovered was that each time the debate at the tables was brought back to the whole floor, the participants were more reluctant to leave the reality of their more intimate, more sustained discussion.

I mention all of this because one of the first messages to be reported from each table to the room as a whole was this: they felt democracy was being seriously undermined by the false urgency so common in the approach of contemporary media. Table after table—without exception—specifically talked about clips and pulsations and short phrases being used as a force which was deforming the reality of democratic public interaction. I was personally surprised, even taken aback. I don't think anybody in the room would have expected that this would be a common theme of the discussion. They seemed to be expressing an undercurrent in public debate. Of course, you can get a false message from a group that takes the trouble to get up on a Saturday morning and comes to take part in a round-table. But I can assure you that it was a very interesting, varied group of people. And they were willing to come together for five hours to discuss extremely interesting subjects. They came from all ages and all backgrounds and all political stripes. What they wanted was real political debate with real time spent. They all seemed to feel that they held this desire in isolation. They were surprised to discover a room filled with citizens

34 who also wanted real debate and who also felt that increasingly high waves of clips and pulsations were not contributing to citizenship and democracy.

All of this relates to something that I've noticed over the past decade or so, since I started going out to talk in halls around the country. I made a conscious decision to do this, rather than take part in endless talking head interviews. It's amazing how much time you free up if you stop going into television studios to give your opinion two or three minutes at a time.

In any case, what I discovered in halls around the country was that citizens do want to come out. They don't simply want to come out to listen, they want to come out in order to be part of a public process which will take some time and will produce ideas; a process focused on the public good. What's more, they come out in very impressive numbers—anything from 500 to 2,000. It's not that they feel each of them must have their turn at the microphone. But they want to be part of a debate which is both corporal and intellectual, as opposed to the disembodied participation that you can get by phoning in to a radio show. I'm not criticizing phone-in shows. At least when you go on them, you can talk with people in an unedited way. All the same, there is that odd phenomenon of people participating without a physical presence. Democracy is dependent on people going into halls and being together. That is what gives them the real freedom to speak and to be heard. It is also what gives a context to what they say. It is a way to measure the courage involved in speaking up. It also limits what is not courage, but the relative self-indulgence of more anonymous interventions. In other words, people coming together in a hall is profoundly democratic because it is about community, about being physically together.

There is something odd though surrounding this phenomenon. I focused on it first in Vancouver some six or seven years ago when I spoke in a hall where there were 2,000 people. In fact, many of them had to be in other halls and followed the conversation by camera relay. I gave my speech and then there was an hour or more of debate. It was probably one of the larger political gatherings to have happened in Vancouver in a long time. What's more, nobody there had been bussed in. Nobody was forced. No one was expected to come. It was simply 2,000 citizens who had decided to come out for an evening to listen to a speech and take part in a debate. The next day, there was absolutely no mention of what had happened anywhere in the media. They had not come and therefore the event had not taken place.

This happens every day across the country. Hundreds, sometimes thousands, of citizens come together. These halls are filled with people for dozens and dozens of reasons. Sometimes it's because

36 there's a well-known speaker. Sometimes it's all about a locally-based question which doesn't involve a particular speaker. They talk among themselves about public issues. They do so outside of the official public debate.

And it is not reported on.

I think that this media silence exists because journalists increasingly see their job as that of reporting on the official structures of power. The idea that there could be something happening outside of the official structures of power simply doesn't play in their surprisingly official view of our means of communication.

What I'm saying is a generalization, but I think I've seen enough of this to have a sense that it represents a pattern. I'm not even specifically suggesting that the media should be reporting on what's said in all of these speeches. But the phenomenon of 500 to 2,000 citizens coming out to spend a full evening discussing the public good is very interesting. Far more interesting than yet another one of those official speeches read by someone who didn't write it and designed to announce something which didn't require a speech.

These people who come voluntarily into halls don't know each other. They sit down in any order and discover each other. They discover that the vice-president of a corporation, sitting next to a student, actually shares a common engagement, even if the two of them disagree on a great deal of what's been discussed. They discover that it is possible to live in a participatory democracy. They realize that this participatory democracy exists in part because people are willing to sit side by side in a hall. What's more, they discover that they want to sit side by side in a hall.

The current methodology of our media, which so often concentrates on scripted emotion or on official statements, means that the public at large does not hear about this very exciting life inside our democracy. We constantly hear that voting numbers are dropping and that we are in desperate need of leadership. We rarely hear that citizens are going out in surprising numbers to be with each other and to talk with each other on a wide variety of subjects. We don't hear that they're giving up a serious percentage of their time to do this.

Where do they find the time? Well, as I have already pointed out, no matter how hard we work, Canadians are living a great deal longer than we've ever lived before. No matter how busy we are, we have more time. And we are the best educated generation ever to have existed. All of that gives us a different sort of access to time. We're curious. And we're actually not in a rush.

This linear, consumer-oriented, insistent society

38 somehow treats us as if we were in a rush. Yet this is our society, so we are treating ourselves as if we were in a rush. How does that contradiction work? I suppose you could say that we are allowing the form of our society to bully the content. Form over content. Directionless structure—which implies a certain innate panic—over the complex meanings of human society.

The pulsation approach towards public communications suggests an astonishing level of urgency. It's as if we're all going to die tomorrow morning, if not overnight. So we must be told certain things 25 times over in summaries of four to six words within the next 12 hours or we may die unsatisfied.

I believe that what actually leads to change inside Western democracy evolves to a great extent in an invisible manner outside of the official process. I believe that it is evolving in good part in these conversations in halls around the country among people who often don't know each other and have no organized relationship with each other. I believe this evolution is the result of people talking to each other in different, informal ways.

These conversations are unheard. That is, they are unheard in the classic sense of the modern exchange of information as it is being conveyed by the media. Conversely, the media has a great deal less influence than most people in public life believe it does. And the more the media ignores these real undercurrents in favour of more official public forms of debate, the less influence it has.

Let me give you an obvious example. In the early 1990s, the NGO movement seemed to appear out of nowhere. Where did it come from? Well, to a great extent, it came out of those halls—out of those unheard conversations—and was therefore completely missed. In fact, it is still not understood because the official way of dealing with it is the old-fashioned media approach of posing questions in an adversarial manner. *Are you for or against what a particular NGO stands for*? No matter how modern the technology being used to pose this question, nothing could be more basic and essentially undemocratic than a Manichaean representation of public debate; that is, the reduction of public debate to the question of *either/or*. In fact, there are hundreds of thousands of young people—anywhere from 15 to 40 years old—who have gone into thousands of different NGOs standing for thousands of different things. It isn't even important to know where you might stand on each of these issues. What would it mean to know where you stood? After all, there are thousands of issues and thousands of nuances. But where did the whole NGO phenomenon come from? That's the real

40 question, the democratic question. And I don't hear it being asked.

Throughout the nineteenth century and the first half of the twentieth century the media, the press, did go into those halls. They went wherever extra-political debates were taking place. What's more, they reported on them in great depth. When a public person went into a hall and spoke on a public issue, even if they had no political role, it was very likely to be reported on at some length in the press. And when citizens gathered in reasonable numbers to talk about issues, it was reported on. Why? For the simple reason that these sorts of gathering were part of the ongoing political, social and democratic process. I can take you back to the speeches of Joseph Howe, many of them given before he was a politician, and show you the lengthy reports in the press. The early speeches of Wilfrid Laurier are the same. Henri Bourassa's speeches. John Dafoe's speeches. There are thousands of examples of this. And they had a direct impact on what 10 or 20 years later would be central to the great debates of public policy.

Let me give you a rather strange example of the disconnect between our concrete reality and what the public are told about. The other day the Secretary General of the United Nations was in Ottawa on a State visit. As part of his visit, he went to the House of Commons to address a joint session of Parliament.

As some of you will know, the Governor General cannot go to the House of Commons. It's been that way since Cromwell. If the Governor General appears in the House of Commons, from a constitutional point of view, it would be an anti-democratic act. So it doesn't happen. On the other hand, the spouse of the Governor General can go to the House of Commons. None of them have done it for a very long time, and so when my office rang up to say that I'd like to be there to hear the Secretary General, most people on the Hill didn't think I was allowed to come. But of course the Speaker knows his history very well and so they all got over their surprise and welcomed me. The only problem was that the seat which used to be reserved for the spouse of the Governor General has long been gone and nobody was clear on exactly where I should be put. In the end I was put in the Speaker's gallery and was very happy to be there.

The point of this story is what I noticed in the House. It was an astonishing scene: the House of the people filled with our members of Parliament, our senators, members of the Privy Council, the diplomatic corps, leaders of the aboriginal community, leaders of the Armed Forces, the Canadians who play a leading role at the international level in the United Nations, the Supreme Court and so on. Every seat in the galleries was filled with people leaning forward with anticipation to see the scene below. Jammed

42 into this large space, which suddenly seemed small, was the combined constituted leadership of Canada. People were turned away. There was absolutely no extra room in the House, except in one section, which was glaringly half empty. Which section? The press box.

Why was the press box half empty? It's more than half empty every day for a very simple reason. The press increasingly follow what happens in the House of Commons through the television monitors in their offices. They don't feel they need to bother to go down to the House.

But the television in the House of Commons follows strict rules and so is only focused on the person who is speaking. There are very good reasons for this. But if you follow what happens in the House of Commons through that camera, then you are getting a very narrow, linear interpretation of what happens in the House.

The word House is appropriate. What is meaningful at any one time may not necessarily be what is being said by the person speaking. It may be the general atmosphere in the House or the reaction of specific people who are not near the person speaking. It may simply be the ability to see who is in the House and who isn't in the House. What's happening off camera is as important as what's happening on camera. Some people are asleep. Some people are furious. Some people are incredulous. Some people are absent.

And so I gazed around the other galleries and then leaned over the balcony and looked down. In my other life I've written novels and it was as if I were transported to a fabulous scene from Zola or Balzac. As the speeches went on, some of the people there became more and more enthusiastic and excited. Other people fell increasingly silent. Some were bored. Some people shrank down into their seats, visibly upset. Some people were thrilled. If you weren't actually there, you missed the democratic phenomenon of the leaders of Canada coming together and experiencing something together. You missed a sense of how it all actually works, what it actually feels like when our leadership are jammed into the same room in order to listen to somebody, an individual who comes in from the outside to talk about something which is relevant to everyone. You missed the opportunity to ask yourself how the hundreds of people in your leadership relate to each other and how they think as a group. It was all there, it was in their faces and in their body language. It was all part of the reality of the democratic process as an expression of community. I could have written a full chapter for a novel or a long analysis for a newspaper on the simple basis of what I saw, as opposed to what I heard.

44   There were some journalists in their seats and they were, to a great extent, those you would expect to find there. I'll leave you to interpret what that phrase actually means. In any case, as a result of the absence of the vast majority of the press corps, I don't think that much of an understanding of what happened in the House that day was communicated to the people of Canada. That's a pity because it was an historic and interesting moment in modern Canada's international role.

PEOPLE WANT to be together. It's a central element of the democratic desire. Nineteenth-century and early twentieth-century false populism deformed part of this through the manipulation of mobs. They removed the beauty from the sense of citizens coming together in a single space. The content of modern false populism remains the same. But it relies on people not being together. The unsatisfiable anger and alienation of the modern version of false populism is dependent upon keeping people apart. In this way their anger cannot be focused and cannot be given a context. This sense of a lack of community drives the anger of individuals, making them feel more inevitably isolated than they are. That in turn gives credence to the false urgency of the pulsations which are put forward as opinions through the disembodied methods of modern communications—that is,

centralized and repetitive communication systems 45
which neither bring people together physically nor
report on people being together.

Now the opinions emitted by these communication systems may not necessarily be inaccurate. But
accuracy is not everything. The meaning of accuracy
comes not from detail but from context. Being right,
if taken out of context, may lead to an unreasonable
or extreme understanding of what is possible. What
makes democracy liveable is that it is based upon the
limiting factors of context. Context is community.

And so any lack of context makes it extremely difficult to carry on a prolonged, intensive debate. It also
makes it very difficult to understand that there may
be a wide variety of opinions or interpretations of
fact inside the body of the community. It may make
it very difficult to make use of the highly valuable
information produced by investigative journalism
inside long-term discussions about public policy.
In other words, debates of public policy are not the
same thing as investigative journalism. They can,
however, be fed by investigative journalism. The
purpose of investigative journalism is not its conclusions. The purpose is the information and the shape
of the information which it provides to the public
debate. That debate will then be able to make sense
of those conclusions, if they are received within a
context—the context of community.

46   Albert Camus said: "Un pays vaut souvent ce que vaut la presse." He was writing in 1944, just after the liberation of France. He was describing the French press of the 1930s, which had been driven by money and self-interest. Having lost its ethical direction, having become the plaything of false populism, it went on almost naturally to become a tool of collaboration under the Vichy regime.

Harry Truman, in one of those wonderful Harry Truman moments, came up to Henry Luce and said, "Mr. Luce, a man like you must have trouble sleeping at night because your job is to inform the people, but what you do is misinform them."

Clifford Sifton was the man who, with Wilfrid Laurier, opened up the West. He was also the owner of the Winnipeg Free Press and thus gave John W. Dafoe the freedom to become a leader of public debate in many areas. Dafoe, through the Free Press and hundreds of public meetings, became, along with another journalist, Henri Bourassa, one of the leaders in the creation of Canadian foreign policy. Clifford Sifton put it that, "It is no part of a newspaper's function to defend a corporation. A corporation is always well able to defend itself." Interestingly enough, Clifford Sifton was one of the richest people in Canada.

It's always interesting to remind ourselves that, whatever the state of our debate on freedom of speech and freedom of the press today, it is in fact the outcome of two centuries of debate in Canada on the nature of freedom of the press.

The slippage towards clips and false urgency is often put down to the simple mechanical needs of modern communication. I don't believe this is a particularly accurate explanation. Equally important, if not more important, is our inability to deal with the flood of facts, the flood of information which overwhelms all of us, whether in the media or not.

If you are an investigative journalist, you're looking for the facts. One of the principal problems is finding the relevant or accurate facts in this unprecedented sea of information. The hard part, even if you have found the accurate or relevant fact, is to find its meaning—that is, the shape in a mountain of apparently shapeless information.

Our societal problem is that there are too many facts and we can't make sense of them. Journalists are regularly shut down by a ton of facts dropping on them. They can't work out their actual sense—certainly not in the time allotted to them.

Traditionally you might think of your job as one of piercing the mountain of secrecy. But in many cases the whole question of secrecy is not all that relevant. Many things seem to be secret, but are actually easily available. They simply can't be identified or given a shape which would reveal their meaning. This prob-

48 lem has been made ever more difficult by the steady rise in specialization over the last hundred years. People who understand particular facts are locked in generic chains of specialization and so are incapable of explaining the shape and meaning of those facts in a language accessible to anybody else. In a sense, they don't really want to make that understanding widely available, because their idea of themselves is tied to the power which comes from their owner-ship of a private language. That is simply one of the characteristics of modern society.

This has lead to an increase in the professional, inward-looking approach towards interpreting facts. Which in turn has led to a romantic phenom-enon—it's something which I wrote about in 1993 in *Voltaire's Bastards*. That romantic phenomenon is the rise of secrecy. A great deal of what is consid-ered secret today has no added value as a secret. This sort of secrecy does not accomplish anything and it is not protecting anything which needs to be protected. It simply adds to the difficulty of giving a shape to facts. This makes it more difficult to carry on a public debate inside a community. Instead, the specialized professions divide our communities up into narrow chimneys filled with people who are incapable of communicating among each other on serious issues. That lack of communication is given credibility by its attribution to the needs of formal secrecy or group loyalty. And so secrecy has become one of the great romantic movements of the last hundred years. If you're looking for signs of this romanticism, you have only to seek out which part of popular literature and entertainment has grown the fastest since the Second World War. You'll probably find it is espionage novels and spy films.

What all this secrecy is about is hard to know. There are very few real secrets. Even armies have almost no real secrets, certainly very few long-term ones. The only secrets which matter in military affairs are short-term secrets related to immediate military actions. In other words, real secrets relate to the time and place of military actions. Secrets relating to weaponry and general information have more to do with self-importance than they do with strategy.

And yet the United States creates about six million new secrets a year. I don't know what the equivalent number would be in other countries. But there is a wonderful irony in the idea that one of the things which the United States government does announce publicly every year is how many secrets it has created.

What could those secrets possibly be? What could their purpose possibly be? What could the purpose

50 of not communicating this information possibly be? How could that possibly add to the functioning of a democratic community?

Let me add one more element to this argument. As we have become more and more professional, and as a larger and larger percentage of the population has fallen into the regular employee category, and particularly into the category of the modern administrative employee, whether in the public sector or the private sector, so the employment contract has grown in importance. It has gone from a simple utilitarian device which regulates work by arbitrating a commercial relationship to one of the most important legal structures determining the freedom of speech of citizens.

People go to university—for example to this university—as a result of taxpayer money and their own money and money they have borrowed and must pay back. They are educated in order to serve themselves as citizens and their society as citizens. You will remember the quotes from Joseph Howe and from the Education Act of British Columbia. People educated themselves in order to become useful citizens within their society. Yet the first thing that happens to them after they graduate, if they are lucky enough to get a job, is that they must sign an employment contract. In that employment contract they turn over the totality of their specialist knowledge to the employer. What's more, they turn over their opinions on that subject to their employer. So, on the one subject on which they are capable of bringing knowledge and expertise to the democratic community table of discussion, the table of public debate, they are immediately silenced through the employment contract. They are only able to speak out publicly on the subjects on which they are not an expert. And so the most educated community in the history of the world has an employment structure which automatically denies citizens the right to contribute to the public debate in a disinterested manner in the areas in which they are particularly knowledgeable. The employment contract is perhaps the single greatest limitation on freedom of speech in Western democracies, yet it is rarely discussed as a limiting factor by the media.

This leads to another point. Because of rising specialization, the resulting administrative opaqueness, as well as the increasing power of the employment contract to silence employees, we began putting in place mechanisms to counteract the growing secrecy. Throughout the democracies, access to information laws were legislated. All of these laws were extremely well intentioned.

However, when we look at them some decades later, we discover that they haven't worked out exactly as we thought they might. Of course, from

52 an investigative journalist's point of view, there are many specific examples of how well the access to information laws can work. However, if you move beyond the specific to the general, you discover that the existence of access to information laws has created the impression that anything which is not specifically acquired through a specific request is automatically inaccessible, if not secret. So that whatever the advantages have been, the access to information methodology has led to the idea that the normal state of affairs is secrecy and that information must specifically be requested. In other words, the normal state of affairs is lack of transparency; and transparency is the result of a professional act—that is, the professional act of a journalist or a politician or a highly motivated citizen making a specific request for information. What's more, there is a financial cost attached to requesting that information; a further barrier to the expectation of normal citizens that transparency ought to be a metaphor for normalcy. It could be argued that the establishment of access to information laws has contributed to the further professionalization of public participation through the professionalization of the use of information. It has thus narrowed our access to information by professionalizing it.

It's almost as if information has importance only if it is thought to be secret. A few days ago a headline in the Ottawa Citizen announced an important revelation: the wonderful architect Douglas Cardinal, who built the Canadian Museum of Civilization, had been lobbying for the building of an aboriginal centre on Victoria Island in the middle of the Ottawa River. The revelation included lists of those he had been lobbying and the costs involved. Altogether this was a sensational bit of information. And it had been produced by an access to information request.

The only thing is, Douglas Cardinal has been trying for the last five years to get anybody who will listen to pay attention to him on this subject. He's been talking everywhere about it. People like myself have been commenting on his plan in speeches on a regular basis for several years. But he hasn't been able to get anybody to report on his wonderful idea. Apparently, the only way it could be reported on was through an access to information request.

You see how these elements fit together. One of Canada's leading architects can give endless speeches calling for something, but it will not be reported on because he is not part of the official process of the management of power. You have to feed that information into the official process for it to be noticed.

THINK ABOUT THESE ISSUES: the tidal waves of facts, the narrow chimneys of specialization, the specialist dialects, the employment con-

54   tract, the rise of secrecy, the misfunction of access to information laws. I suppose you could describe all of this as a confusion between the importance and debate of ideas as opposed to the importance of the eternal chase for facts. We need both. But democracies are driven by ideas because ideas are about the sense of direction. The facts may provide a sense of urgency. But the facts won't save you. And the facts won't give you the possibility of a direction.

Joseph Howe, Louis LaFontaine, Robert Baldwin, Charles Tupper—that's what they are all about. They are about ideas and debating ideas and convincing the citizenry and their community of these ideas and then winning a mandate to put those ideas into effect. That is the democratic process. If you don't have the debate of ideas, you don't have a democracy.

So, our obsession with facts and our difficulty in dealing with facts and giving a shape to facts is making it more and more difficult to engage in a debate of ideas. I'm convinced that the difficulty we have in reporting on the lengthy debates taking place every night in halls around the country is tied to the facility with which facts can be reported on. Ideas are just words in this current atmosphere. Facts, on the other hand, seem important because they can be measured.

ONE FINAL POINT. It was announced a decade or so ago that we were entering into a third or fourth industrial revolution. It was going to be a revolution in ideas. As a result, we were entering into the knowledge economy. And countries like Canada were going to do well because we have high levels of education and we have universities and we have ideas. As a result, we were going to be able to live off the knowledge economy, just as we had lived off selling car parts, and before that off wheat. We were going to be able to live off the royalties earned from licensing our ideas. Therefore, we had to broaden and strengthen and lengthen copyright and intellectual property laws.

Curiously enough, nobody said, *Hold on a minute. What you're proposing is that in a society based upon democracy, that is to say based upon freedom of speech, that is to say based upon the free exchange of ideas, we are going to build an economy that is based upon selling the exclusive right to ideas to individual corporations. And as a result of their purchase they will have control over those ideas and over the language surrounding them. Therefore, what you are intending to do is to build our economy upon the limitation of ideas and therefore of freedom of speech.*

That could have led to an interesting discussion. But not only was there no discussion, there is *still* no discussion. And already the idea of the knowledge economy is breaking down. It simply isn't possible

56 to maintain community cohesion at the same time as a radical expansion in the limitation of the public transferral of ideas. You can see this impossibility, for example, around the pharmaceutical question. The ownership of intellectual property over drugs has a certain logic to it. But does that logic extend to allowing people to die from AIDS because they cannot afford access to drugs, the prices of which are established thanks to intellectual property legislation? And can you maintain the intellectual property/maximum price symbiosis when it leads to poverty among older people, particularly in a society where there are more and more older people?

For those people who do not live in one of the 20 Western democracies, the effect of the knowledge economy is to create a postmodern version of the absentee landlords of the nineteenth century. You'll remember this from your high-school days. There were absentee landlords living in London whose wealth came from the income they earned from their ownership of property in Ireland. There's no difference between the disorder which this Irish poverty caused, and our current situation, in which educated people in the Western democracies own ideas, the outcomes of which have to be bought by people who can't afford them in the developing world. This is postmodern absentee landlordism. It is a fundamental intellectual problem for democracy.

O UR DISCOMFORT with this whole range of limitations can be seen through the increasing pressure for whistle-blower protection legislation. And it is a wonderful thing that such pressure is growing. But that doesn't deal with the fundamental situation. I've been attempting to describe to you some of the underlying themes of our society: Everything is assumed to be secret unless it is specifically requested. We have professional languages which do not have as their purpose communication. Loyalty to your employer is more important than the obligation of citizenship. And so on. You cannot change this fundamental situation through specific legislation dealing with access to information or the protection of whistle-blowers. You can chip away at it. But you can't change it that way.

This is one of those fascinating moments in a civilization when you need to have a fundamental debate in order to get at the roots of what is happening. That is quite different from reacting in a specific manner in order to alleviate the effects of what is happening. If we do not give ourselves the right to have that fundamental debate, we could find ourselves locked in a process which is destructive to our democracy.

Let me finish with one last example. A few days ago there was a public meeting in Ottawa which brought together 70 or so organizations—universi-

58 ties, cities, libraries, government organizations, etc. This meeting was organized by PEN Canada and PEN Quebec. It was aimed at creating a network across Canada for writers in exile. Its purpose, in other words, was to create a network which would allow us to bring a reasonable number of writers into Canada who would be in danger if they stayed in their countries; and not simply to bring them to Canada, but to bring them to Canada in a context which would allow them to build a new life.

This sort of network already exists in Sweden, Norway, Germany and in parts of the United States. I believe this is an important initiative. The South African writer, Antjie Krog, when covering the Truth and Reconciliation Commission in her country, described herself as being stunned by the knowledge of the price people had paid for their words. Most of us have little real sense of what that means. We make it real by creating real places for some of these people in Canada.

The meeting in Ottawa was announced to the press. There were even three journalists taking part on their own time. And yet there was no representation there from the media. I'm not criticizing. I'm just a little disappointed. John Fraser, who is here with us, was also there. Why? Because Massey College, of which he is Master, had taken a lead in this area by making space for several exiled writers. I believe they now have four spots. There are another two at George Brown College and one at the Banff Centre. Now, this is an initiative which needs to be talked about publicly, because the state of freedom of speech elsewhere in the world is relevant to the state of freedom of speech in Canada. If ours is stronger than elsewhere, well then, we owe something to people elsewhere, people who are dying in order to save or strengthen their freedom of speech. They are much more on the line than any one of us, no matter how difficult our situation might be. The creation of such a network is therefore one of those rare opportunities when we can not only put our money where our mouth is, but also our energies.

So I do hope that, as the work goes on towards the creation of this national network, the press will become interested and will talk about it and indeed will find places within their organizations to welcome some of these writers in exile.

L ET ME COME BACK to the many journalism students here in this room. I don't know what you're studying at this moment in your classes. But you could do worse than simply to read the Charter of Rights. If you have read it, re-read it. How could you think about being journalists if you have not

60   read the Charter of Rights or read it thinking about what it means to you as a journalist? Read again the four fundamental freedoms. Read in particular lines nine and ten.

The definition of our second fundamental freedom begins by talking about the freedom of thought—notice it begins with thought, not facts—and goes on to belief, opinion and expression. Ask yourself what that means. Does this definition simply describe our freedom to write and express our thoughts, beliefs, opinions and expressions? Or does it also include our right to hear thoughts, beliefs, opinions and expressions? And does the right to hear thoughts, like the right to think, not implicitly include the right to hear a variety of thoughts? Most citizens do not become journalists or writers. Few of us will have lengthy and sustained opportunities to speak and be heard. But we do have the right to hear. It is one of the ways in which we will feed the debates in our personal lives. That is our democratic right. We—all citizens—have the right to hear a variety of opinions and we all have the right to hear a varied debate.

Argument, variety of opinion, context, the shape of ideas, a core of ethics—those are all things which Joseph Howe understood. Those are the elements which shaped his career. As the man himself put it:

> My public life is before you and I know you will believe me when I say that when I sit down in solitude to the

labours of my profession, the only questions I ask myself   61
are: what is right, what is just, what is for the public good?
I am of no party, but I hold that when I am performing
my duty to the country, I am sincerely doing that which I
engaged to do when I took the press into my hands.

1   3   5   7   6   4   2

Library and Archives Canada Cataloguing in Publication

Saul, John Ralston, 1947–
Joseph Howe & the battle for freedom of speech
/ John Ralston Saul.
ISBN 1-55447-019-6 (BOUND)
ISBN 1-55447-018-8 (PBK.)
1. Howe, Joseph, 1804-1873. 2. Freedom of speech—Canada.
3. Freedom of the press—Canada. 4. Freedom of information
— Canada. 5. Intellectual property—Canada. 6. Press—
Canada. 7. Democracy—Canada. I. Title.
FC2322.1.H6S27 2006 323.44'3'0971 C2005-907347-0

GASPEREAU PRESS LIMITED
Gary Dunfield & Andrew Steeves
Printers & Publishers
47 Church Avenue, Kentville, Nova Scotia
Canada B4N 2M7 *www.gaspereau.com*